DEATH ROW'S ODDEST INMATES

Ty Treadwell

Copyright © 2012 Ty Treadwell

All rights reserved.

ISBN: 1477450653
ISBN-13: 978-1477450659

"Laughing on the way to your execution is not generally understood by less advanced life-forms, and they'll call you crazy."
—Richard Bach

"I am for the death penalty. Who commits terrible acts must get a fitting punishment. That way he learns the lesson for the next time."
—Britney Spears

CONTENTS

Introduction	7
Robert Vickers	10
Monty Delk	16
James Paster	21
Spotlight On: Wacky Weapons	25
Pernell Ford	34
Daniel Colwell	39
James Kelly Moss	45
Spotlight On: Jailhouse Jokers	51
Horace Kelly	55
Christopher Newton	61
Charles Singleton	66
Spotlight On: Laughable Lawsuits	71
Varnall Weeks	76

Aileen Wuornos	82
Spotlight On: Massive Last Meals	90
Stanley Baker Jr.	95
Edwin Hart Turner	99
Spotlight On: Loony Last Words	105

Introduction

Every social group has one member who's a little off. Maybe their sense of humor is a bit edgy, a bit inappropriate. Maybe they talk too loud, smile too wide, or have a strange look in their eyes. They might have bizarre hobbies and interests, or use words you've never heard before. One minute they make you laugh, the next minute they make you nervous.

In school, it's the class clown. At work, it's the office prankster. And despite the gloomy surroundings, every death row cell block has at least one oddball as well. Some of them goof off, act silly, and make nonstop wisecracks. Others have a dry, more sophisticated sense of humor. Some are amazingly articulate. Others ramble and rant like a mystic yogi on LSD. Some are regarded as flawed geniuses. Others are just flawed.

So if a convict cracks jokes about their own impending execution, does that make them totally warped or just a little weird? If a prisoner invents their own language or discusses space ships and time travel, should we consider them brilliant or brain-damaged?

It would be easy to simply label them all insane, but that would be a broad and inaccurate conclusion. Insanity is a highly popular defense strategy—especially during murder trials—but it's often used as a last-ditch effort when every other legal appeal has failed. Some killers do have past histories of mental instability, but others only show signs of dementia after spending countless years in prison.

Psychiatric experts have also pointed out that while it's nearly impossible for an insane criminal to fake being sane, a sane criminal can pretend to be deranged without much effort. One of the most famous cases of this involved David Berkowitz, the serial killer known as Son of Sam. In court, Berkowitz claimed that a demon who took the form of a black dog instructed him to murder his six victims. Less than two years after he was convicted and given a 25-to-life sentence, Berkowitz admitted that he made up the stories about demons and dogs.

In a reverse situation, lawyers for Unabomber Theodore Kaczynski thought an insanity plea would help their client avoid a death sentence, but Kaczynski—whose mail bomb campaign killed three people and wounded 23 others—refused to go along and swore that he was mentally sound when he committed his crimes.

So what's the verdict on all those jailhouse jesters whooping it up in their cells? Are they clever and cunning, or just plain peculiar? The jury's still out on whether it's creative genius or malfunctioning brain matter that fuels their actions, but one thing's for certain; despite the lack of sunshine, fresh air, and other pleasantries of daily life, there's apparently no shortage of silliness and outlandish behavior on death row.

Robert Vickers

The inventive skills of Thomas Edison. The resourcefulness of MacGyver. And the poor spelling ability of a slightly dim first grader. Put them all together, add a dash of humor and a spoonful of psychotic rage, and you've got Robert Vickers—or "Bonzai Bob," as he was known in the prison circuit.

Vickers began his life of crime at an early age; he developed a fondness for stabbing other children with pencils, and was arrested for the first time while still in sixth grade. As a teenager, Vickers turned his attention to theft. He once committed 12 burglaries in a 13-day period and confessed to dozens more while in custody. But it wasn't until Vickers entered the prison system that his criminal rampage truly began.

After being jailed for grand theft at age 19, Vickers added another 10 to 15 years to his sentence by stabbing a fellow inmate. Shortly afterward, Vickers was given a new roommate; convicted killer Frank Ponciano. The arrangement lasted less than two weeks.

One day while Vickers was napping, guards delivered lunch trays to the cell. Ponciano failed to wake Vickers up, and also drank the Kool-Aid from the other man's tray. Vickers was so enraged that he strangled Ponciano with a bed sheet then stabbed him with a homemade shank made from a sharpened toothbrush. Once Ponciano was dead, Vickers used the shank to carve *bonzai*—a misspelled version of the famous Japanese war cry—into the other man's back.

At least he didn't spell it *bonsai*. There's nothing less badass than those tiny little trees.

"Bonzai Bob" then yelled for the guards, saying "Get this stinking son of a bitch out of my cell! I think he died last night." The guards were wary, but when Vickers started poking Ponciano with a lit cigar to prove he was dead, they entered the cell to inspect the body.

Vickers openly confessed his crime to the prison psychologists. He admitted to strangling and stabbing Ponciano and said his only regret was that he didn't have time to dot the *i* with a swastika when he carved *bonzai* into the other man's flesh.

Vickers wasn't upset when he was sentenced to death for the crime. In fact, he seemed eager to die and wondered why the state was taking so long to execute him. "What's the hold up, fella?" he wrote in a letter to the governor. "If ya don't do it soon, I'm gonna draw more blood than your cheap mops can absorb. I'm a very impatient person. I never did like waiting. I've got a date with the devil's wife!"

After his transfer to death row, Vickers became even more of a troublemaker. The wily killer was both clever and double-jointed, enabling him to escape from handcuffs and holding cells. He attacked guards and fellow inmates whenever he had the chance, and he had a knack for creating makeshift weapons from anything he could get his hands on. He could turn nearly any object into a knife, and he once stabbed a guard with a spear made from typewriter parts and rolled-up newspapers.

Vickers also escaped from his death row cell one night by shorting out the electronic lock then climbing through an air vent to the prison roof. Once he got there, though, he realized that he was too high up to jump. After performing a striptease for a nearby female guard, Vickers was roughly escorted back to his cell.

Less than a day before Vickers was scheduled to die in Arizona's gas chamber, a district judge granted him a stay of execution. Vickers went nuts and told reporters that he hoped somebody "snuffed the judge's mama." He also vowed to carve the judge's name in his next victim if the state didn't execute him soon.

To speed up the process, Vickers decided to add a second murder victim to his long list of offenses. Buster Holsinger, another death row inmate, had once made a rude remark about Vickers's niece, so Vickers made a Molotov Cocktail by filling an empty ice cream carton with hair tonic, stuffing a strip of toilet paper inside, then lighting the crude device on fire. He tossed it into Buster's cell, then squirted more hair tonic through the bars when the flames didn't seem high enough.

The entire death row block had to be evacuated because of the smoke, which nearly killed all the other inmates. When a guard asked Vickers what happened, he calmly replied, "I burned Buster." The guard then asked if Buster was dead, and Vickers said, "He should be. He's on fire."

Vickers received yet another death sentence for murdering Buster Holsinger, and was promptly confined to his cell. The bars were covered with a sheet of thick plastic to keep Vickers from throwing out bodily waste or stabbing anyone who happened to walk by. "Bonzai Bob" spent his final days writing letters to the governor and other state officials, always using a swastika to dot the *i* in his nickname.

In one letter, Vickers asked if his last meal could be prepared by a woman. He also requested permission to wear a 3-piece suit to his execution. "I wanna die dressed," he wrote. "Gonna be some ladies there. I don't wanna go nude or in state clothes."

Both requests were denied, but Vickers did receive his chosen last meal—green chili burros, burritos with barbecued steak, French fries, vanilla ice cream, cream soda, and a cigarette.

Prison officials breathed a sigh of relief once Vickers was strapped down to the lethal injection table. (By the time Vickers was executed in 1999, lethal injection had replaced the gas chamber as Arizona's instrument of death.) The condemned man seemed pretty cheerful as well, smiling at his relatives and calling out, "Hello everybody. See you later!"

After the execution, the other death row inmates were finally able to relax, too. Now that "Bonzai Bob" had uttered his final *sayonara*, their maximum security cell block was once again a calm, quiet place to live.

Monty Delk

Who was Monty Delk? Well, that depends on who you ask. Police and prosecutors labeled him as a clever, manipulative killer. Fellow death row inmates described Delk as smart and educated. Prison psychiatrists and Delk's own attorney believed Delk was mentally incompetent and possibly insane.

And if you asked Delk himself, he would have told you he was a doctor, a police chief, a submarine captain, or a zombie, depending on what day it was.

From an early age, Monty Delk was a man you wouldn't want to work with, or be married to, or get within 50 yards of. As a teenager, Delk made death threats against a co-worker at a lumber mill and another co-worker at a Pizza Hut. He routinely beat his young wife, although he also tried to recruit her as his partner in crime. The former wife had this to say at Delk's trial:

"Well, he looked through the paper, and he would see an ad for something like a ring, a diamond ring, worth a lot of money; and the plan was we would go to their house, say we were married and everything, see how many people were in the house, and hold them at gunpoint, tie them up, take their valuables, shoot them in the head, and leave."

Delk's wife smartly vetoed the idea, but that didn't stop Delk from trying the plan on his own. Having just lost his Volkswagen in a card game, Delk saw a newspaper ad for a used Chevy Camaro and went to the owner's house to see the car in person. The owner, Gene "Bubba" Allen, offered to take Delk for a test drive. During that ill-fated ride, Delk murdered Allen with a shotgun blast to the head, dumped his body in a ditch, and stole the car. When Delk was caught four days later, he was still in possession of both the car and the murder weapon. He also had a photo of his victim's wife in his wallet, which prosecutors claim "showed very bad judgment on his part."

Delk was summarily tried, convicted, and given a death sentence—but after several years on death row, the killer began to say and do odd things. He babbled constantly. He uttered bizarre statements. His supposed identity changed from moment to moment. Delk claimed to be a policeman, a judge, a federal agent, a prison warden, the king of England, the president of Kenya, a commando, and a congressman. He once signed his name as "Vito Corleone" and told tales about his adventures aboard a nuclear-powered submarine during the Civil War. He gave his age as 50, or 99, or 129, and claimed that he had been married 95 million years earlier.

"I was born old," he explained.

The nuttier Delk acted, the less attention he paid to personal hygiene. He rarely took showers, and when he did, he refused to use soap or remove his clothes. Delk's body odor grew so bad that he had to be segregated from other inmates to keep them from becoming nauseous.

"I think he's bonkers," remarked Delk's attorney, who clarified that statement with a more clinical description. "He has long periods of psychotic thought punctuated by grandiose delusions, incoherent ramblings, and smearing himself with his own feces, interspersed with brief moments of lucidity and compliance."

The general opinion was that years of confinement and a bad reaction to prison medicine had turned

Delk's brain into mush. He was labeled bipolar and treated with special care. Delk's new lawyer tried to get the death sentence commuted on the grounds that Delk was too mentally unstable to be executed. But many in the legal system weren't buying it.

"He's crazy like a fox," said one member of the sheriff's department. "If anybody needs a needle stuck in his arm, that dude's the one who needs it."

"He is a faker," added a local district attorney. "He'll slip up occasionally with inmates, other personnel, and show his true colors."

A prison employee claimed he heard Delk tell another inmate that he had been "playing the crazy fool" to avoid a death sentence. The state pointed out that Delk seemed perfectly normal during his trial, and that he "finds it in his best interest to appear incompetent when an audience is available." Delk had shown signs of high intelligence and cunning while in prison, including times when he would eavesdrop on prison employees and memorize the names of their wives, their children, and even their license plate numbers in order to make personalized threats.

The attempt to spare Delk's life with an insanity defense ultimately failed. While the Supreme Court won't allow an insane person to be executed, they also don't define what constitutes "insane." To them, Delk was just as sane as any other psychotic, delusional, incoherent, feces-smeared person.

The state of Texas executed Delk on February 28, 2002. Delk wasn't happy about the situation, and he kicked and screamed all the way to the lethal injection table. His last words were a rambling string of obscenities followed by threats and insults. "I am the warden of this unit!" Delk shouted. "Get your warden off this gurney and shut up! You are not in America. This is the island of Barbados. People will see you doing this!"

When asked for their reaction later that day, the population of Barbados reportedly replied, "Excuse me? Monty who?"

James Paster

One person described James Paster as "Satan personified." Another called him "a sick, sick individual who had no respect for humanity." A kindly 74-year-old woman remarked, "He doesn't deserve to be on this Earth."

What type of vile, disgusting monster could prompt scathing insults like this? Yes, that's right. James Paster was—a lounge singer.

Of course, he also participated in multiple rapes and murders. Maybe that's what people were referring to. But you have to admit it—nobody likes a lounge singer.

Paster's life of crime began at an early age. He was jailed multiple times on a variety of charges, including raping his own mother and sister when he was 16 years old. When he wasn't in prison, Paster bounced between different jobs including cook, rock musician, Elvis impersonator, and a one-time stint as a professional hit man.

In 1980, lady truck driver Trudy Howard hired Paster and two accomplices to kill her husband, Robert Earl Howard, so she could collect the insurance money. Paster pulled the trigger himself, but then urged his two accomplices to kill someone so they would all be "even." A few weeks after the hired hit, the three men raped and killed a 27-year-old woman. The trio later abducted a teenage girl whose car had broken down on the side of the road. The girl was raped and strangled with an electrical cord before Paster drove a nail up her nose to make sure she was dead.

Paster was eventually arrested and charged with multiple counts of rape and murder, earning a death sentence for the contract killing of Robert Howard. While in custody, Paster spoke casually about his crimes. He admitted that he and his two accomplices were paid $1000 and given a used motorcycle for shooting Howard, and remarked that killing strangers was an easy thing to do. "Had I ever known this individual, had a drink or a beer with him, I wouldn't have done it. (Not knowing him) made it easier, like hitting someone on the highway.

It's not hard to take a life. One shot, 20 feet away, in the head."

Paster claimed to not remember much about the rapes and murders of the two young women. When police asked how the teenage girl was dressed when Paster and his friends abducted her, Paster only sneered and said "Man, she was just some girl that was going to die, and you want me to remember what she was wearing?"

Although he freely confessed to all of his crimes, Paster also fought his conviction with a series of flimsy appeals. At one point, he earned a reprieve from his scheduled execution when his lawyers argued that the bologna sandwiches Paster was served during his trial were nutritionally lacking, robbing their client of adequate strength to defend himself in court.

Paster also argued that since the jail was "quite a distance" from the courthouse, he had to get up early in the morning in order to make his court appearances and therefore never got a good night's sleep. He later complained that his shoulder began hurting as he sat in the courtroom one day during his trial, but no one did anything about it.

When the whining and lame excuses failed to save his life, Paster took more proactive measures. One evening after the lights on death row were turned out, Paster and his cellmate Nobel Mays put dummies in their bunks, slathered themselves from head to toe with hair tonic, then managed to squeeze through a tiny air vent into a utility corridor behind their cell wall. The two were in the process of sawing their way through an exhaust fan with a hacksaw when they were caught by prison guards.

"You can't blame a guy for trying," Paster said afterwards. "I'm about as smart as a box of rocks." Prison officials probably should have been wary of Paster right from the start. At one point during his incarceration, the inmate expressed a desire to study mining engineering. "You never know when a tunnel's going to come in handy," he explained.

Any future escape attempts were avoided when Paster was executed on September 20, 1989. Despite the brutality of his crimes and the scathing comments others made about him, Paster went to his death with a high opinion of himself. In a pre-execution interview, Paster was asked how he would like to be remembered. His reply? "One hell of a lot of fun. If you knew me, I would be an unforgettable character. I'm a very likeable individual."

Spotlight On: Wacky Weapons

When it comes to murder weapons, knives and guns have always shared the most popularity. But in moments of rare creativity—or perhaps simple desperation—some killers have found tools, sports equipment, and common household items to be equally adept at taking lives.

After knives and guns, tools show up the most often on lists of murder weapons. In addition to fearsome items like hatchets and ice picks, the contents of your average tool box make frequent guest appearances at crime scenes. In fact, so many hammers, wrenches, and screwdrivers have been used in homicides that Home Depot might want to start running background checks and requiring a 5-day waiting period on its more "murder-friendly" items.

Although they're not nearly as light and portable, yard tools and construction equipment are often used for nefarious purposes, too. Jeffrey Cook was convicted of killing his sister with a sledgehammer because she stayed longer than he wanted her to during a visit. Luis Rosales Rivera also used a sledgehammer to murder his roommate because the other man was too bossy and forced Rivera to clean the bathroom. Yashesh Desai was accused of killing his father with a weed trimmer, but was declared unfit to stand trial. And pre-trial motions are currently underway for Stephen Shappell, accused of bludgeoning his lover's husband to death with a shovel after spiking the victim's Snapple drink with poison. By the way, could it merely be a coincidence that when you combine "shovel" with "Snapple," you get "Shappell?" I think not.

Strangulation is another popular murder method, and killers have used a wide variety of objects to do the deed including ropes, scarves, stockings, shoelaces, belts, chains, and telephone cords. William Murray, executed in Texas, strangled a 93-year-old woman with an Ace bandage. Thomas Grasso, executed in Oklahoma, strangled an 87-year-old woman with a string of lights taken from her own Christmas tree.

When it comes to sports equipment, the baseball bat remains world champion of impromptu weapons.

But over the years, killers have discovered that anything that can be swung—including tennis racquets and hockey sticks—can also be used as an instrument of death. Dion Smallwood, executed in Oklahoma, even used a croquet mallet to kill his girlfriend's mother. But after the baseball bat, the sports weapon of choice seems to be the golf club—and every club in the bag, from drivers to short irons, has been an accessory to murder at some point.

Steven DeMocker, awaiting a retrial after his first one ended in a mistrial, has been accused of using a 7-wood to kill his ex-wife. Alison Gorrie admitted to beating her own son to death with a putter, and Gordon Franklin used the same club to kill his daughter. Robert Lowry struck and killed a fellow teenager with a 5-iron during a brawl, and Julie Travis was convicted of killing her son with a 6-iron during a drunken rage. The most infamous golf club murder of all, however, involved Kennedy relative Michael Skakel. Skakel, the nephew of Senator Robert F. Kennedy's widow, also chose a 6-iron to kill teenaged neighbor Martha Moxley.

Some killers have a flair for the exotic. Eddie Trice, executed in Oklahoma, beat his 84-year-old victim to death with a pair of nunchucks. Richard Martin is serving time in England for using the same weapon to kill a fellow teenager outside a "Pimps and Hookers"-themed Halloween party in 2007. Porn actor Stephen Hill used a movie prop sword to kill fellow porn actor Herbert Wong, AKA Tom Dong. Hill fell to his death as he tried to escape from police. Australian John Sharpe was jailed in 2005 for murdering his wife and daughter with a spear gun. In 2010, Zhou Fang of Canada was charged with first-degree murder after he shot and killed his father with a crossbow inside a library. And Michael Desiderio was sentenced to 15 years in prison for killing another teen with a samurai sword after the two argued over a pillow. If only the situation had been reversed, and the two had argued over a samurai sword before getting into a pillow fight.

In the heat of passion, even the most common household item can become a deadly weapon. Christopher Emmett, executed in Virginia, beat a coworker to death with a brass lamp. Rogelio Cannady, executed in Texas, was serving time for two other murders when he beat his cellmate to death with a padlock. Teen Daniel Kovarbasich was found guilty of voluntary manslaughter after he hit an older man in the head with a gallon-sized jar of pickles before stabbing him over 50 times with a knife. Ronald Weed used a ceramic statue of an Indian to bludgeon his mother and niece to death. A bowling trophy was the murder weapon of choice for Mercedes Smith, convicted of bludgeoning an elderly neighbor. Lovers Patricia Columbo and Frank DeLuca also used a bowling trophy when they killed Columbo's parents and brother.

One disturbing recent trend is the use of vacuum cleaners as murder weapons. In England, Stephen Hotson beat his wife to death with their vacuum cleaner then tried to kill himself—by jumping out of a first-floor window. In Florida, Gregory McGruder Jr. used a vacuum cleaner, beer bottle, and chair leg when he bludgeoned his girlfriend to death. Nebraska resident Monique Lee strangled her ex-landlord to death with a vacuum cleaner cord because she was angry about being evicted. And in South Carolina, Tina Pressley struck her common-law husband with a vacuum cleaner, knocking him unconscious, then finished the job by choking him. Police noted that "some of the vacuum's attachments might also have been involved."

Sometimes it's the method of murder and not the weapon that's unusual. Alan Matheney killed his ex-wife with a shotgun, and John Peoples Jr. used a rifle to kill three people—but in both cases, the whole "point and shoot" procedure was obviously too complicated, because both men beat their victims to death with the guns. I can picture those two sitting side by side in the prison cafeteria, eating soup with the wrong end of the spoon and wondering why it's taking so long to get to the bottom of the bowl.

When it comes to odd murder weapons, though, Phillip Wilkinson definitely ranks near the top of the list. Wilkinson led a strange double life, apparently stuck between the extremes of good and evil with no idea which way to turn. Wilkinson's parents divorced when he was six, leaving Phillip and his brother and sister in the care of their mother, a licensed nurse. The mother was a fundamentalist Pentecostal who didn't care for work, so the family moved from one temporary shelter to another while depending on donations from various churches.

Wilkinson's mother urged all of her children to participate in Pentecostal rituals such as testifying and speaking in tongues. She answered the phone by saying, "Praise the Lord" instead of "Hello," and didn't allow her children to trick-or-treat on Halloween because of the holiday's dubious origins. If costumed children came to her house, she handed out religious pamphlets instead of candy.

Wilkinson grew up hating his mother, but his religious upbringing obviously left a lasting impression. As a young man in the Army, Wilkinson preached to his fellow soldiers about hell, the devil, and the dangers of earthly temptations—but whenever he had free time, he would drink heavily and wander through neighborhoods looking for windows with open curtains, hoping to spy a woman undressing or a couple having sex.

One night, Wilkinson met a female friend for drinks at a local restaurant. He consumed roughly ten beers and six mixed drinks during the meeting, then got angry at his lady friend because she had been "teasing" and "flirtatious." When the woman left the bar, Wilkinson followed in his car with the intent to rape her. A barking dog scared Wilkinson away from the woman's home, though, and he eventually found himself in an apartment complex near his army barracks. As he sneaked through the complex in the dark, he looked through a sliding glass door and saw a teenage girl asleep on a sofa in one of the apartments. Wilkinson became excited, and when he noticed a bowling pin outside the apartment door, he suddenly knew that he had to kill the girl.

Personally, I've never seen a bowling pin anywhere outside of a bowling alley. If most people saw one outside someone's apartment, their first thought would be, "How in the world did that get there?" as opposed to "This is a sign that I must commit murder!" Unfortunately, Wilkinson's mind took the road less traveled.

With the bowling pin in hand, Wilkinson crept inside the apartment and began to fondle the teenager. She woke up and tried to fight her attacker, and that's when Wilkinson hit her with the bowling pin. He would later confess that he "just kept bopping her…like 70 times." He then tried to sexually assault the girl, but couldn't achieve an erection. Wilkinson searched the apartment and found the girl's mother and brother, also asleep. He bludgeoned them with the bowling pin as well, then used a light bulb to sexually assault both of the women.

The three murders went unsolved for six months until Wilkinson—still torn between his evil urges and his religious zeal—turned himself in and confessed to the crimes. He was sentenced to death, a punishment Wilkinson gladly accepted and never challenged in court. But before the sentence could be carried out, legal insanity burst onto the scene.

Barely 24 hours before his scheduled execution in 1997, prison guards found two suicide notes in

Wilkinson's cell. The execution was halted, because even though it's legal for an inmate to accept their death sentence, the fact that Wilkinson considered killing himself before the state could kill him made the court question his mental state. By their logic, a man who contemplates suicide might be too unstable to understand his legal rights, including the right to appeal his execution—something Wilkinson never did.

Phillip Wilkinson remains on death row to this day. Maybe the courts will *spare* his life, but hopefully this killer will never have the chance to *strike* again. At least he confessed to his crimes and didn't try to *frame* someone else. Still, the guy's a real *turkey*.

Pernell Ford

And now for the next round in our popular quiz series, "Auto Dealership or Convicted Killer?" The question is, "Pernell Ford." And the answer is—yes, you guessed it; convicted killer.

At age six, when most kids are entering school, Pernell Ford found himself entering a mental institution. By age 13, he was taking powerful anti-psychotic and anti-depressant medication. And by 18, he had committed the crime that would earn him a death sentence.

On December 2, 1983, Ford entered the home of 74-year-old Willie Griffith and her 42-year-old daughter Linda to commit a burglary. Ford thought the house was empty, but was surprised to find the two women at home. When Linda tried to prevent Ford from escaping, he stabbed her to death. He also stabbed the elderly and disabled Willie Griffith to death because she was, in Ford's words, "raising so much Cain."

Linda Griffith once worked as a secretary for a renowned German rocket scientist, but no one needed her former boss's help to solve the murders. Pernell Ford was arrested the next day while driving his victim's car and wearing blood-spattered clothing, and it didn't take a rocket scientist to figure out that he was guilty as hell.

Not only did Ford give police a complete confession, but he was also allowed to act as his own attorney—despite the fact that he was only 18 and had an IQ of 80, a limited education, and a long history of mental problems. Ford showed up in court wearing a toga made from bed sheets and towels, then gave a rambling speech describing the supernatural powers imparted on him by God. Ford claimed that he could teleport himself anywhere in the world by a method he called "translation." He had supposedly used this power to travel to countries such as India, Ecuador, Spain, Colombia, and the Philippines, and had amassed 400,000 wives and countless children in those countries. He also claimed to have millions of dollars in a Swiss bank account which could support his many wives and children while he was in jail.

Ford might have had a flair for storytelling and homemade costume design, but his legal skills paled in comparison. While acting as his own attorney, he chose to use the daring but rarely successful "resurrection defense." Ford asked the judge to bring the coffins of his victims into the court room so that God could bring them back to life, therefore nullifying any murder charges against him.

The judge politely declined and sentenced Ford to death, adding that the killer would receive an automatic appeal. Ford said he didn't want one, and claimed that he was looking forward to his death so he could sit at God's left hand and become part of the Holy Trinity. As he left the courtroom, he waved and called out, "See you at the electric chair!"

Because of Ford's bizarre courtroom behavior, he was subjected to numerous psychological tests to determine if he was sane enough to be executed. Three different mental health professionals found Ford to be completely competent and added that Ford was, at most, just a little antisocial. They claimed that he "was not, and presently is not, insane, incompetent, or suffering from any thought or mood disorder." One court-appointed psychiatrist estimated Ford's real IQ to be closer to 110 than 80, and said that Ford was "perfectly capable of knowing what to do to beat the system or confuse the system."

Another stated that Ford's plan to become part of the Holy Trinity wasn't delusional, but only a creative interpretation. He said, "Ford believes in the afterlife that he is going to have a cherished position in heaven, that he is going to be respected, and that he is going to be comfortable and happy there." He also added that Ford "doesn't have the educational or philosophical background, perhaps, to take more than a fairly direct interpretation of the Bible. I mean, he is not a Biblical scholar by any means, but he is a person under stress who is turning to religion for support, and particularly because he doesn't have other kinds of support available to him."

Pernell Ford agreed with their assessments, saying "I had a lot of problems when I was little, but nothing that can classify me as insane."

On June 2, 2000, Ford was executed in Alabama's electric chair, affectionately dubbed "Yellow Mama" because it's painted with the same bright yellow paint used by the State Highway Department to paint lines on local roads. Prior to his death, Ford enjoyed a last meal of barbecued ribs, ham, English peas, turnip greens, potato salad, cornbread, and cheesecake. For his final statement, Ford read Bible passages and apologized to the family of his victims.

Little did the executioner know that as he pulled the switch, he was creating 400,000 widows all at once.

Daniel Colwell

Not all death row inmates have tattoos, scars, bulging muscles, and a cold stare that could frighten the paint off a wall. Daniel Colwell was referred to as a "gentle giant," a man over six feet tall and 300 pounds but with a soft voice and a smile that could light up a room. Even the judge who sentenced Colwell to death called him "a witty, friendly guy." But like everyone else on death row, Colwell was sent there for a reason; the premeditated murder of two innocent people.

The motive? Colwell wanted to die, but his many suicide attempts had been unsuccesful. He then decided to kill someone else so he would receive the death penalty. But not just any murder victim would do; Colwell, who was black, thought a white victim would increase his chances of being sentenced to death. He also calculated that two murders instead of one would boost the odds even further.

Colwell bought a gun and drove to his local Wal-Mart, then sat in the parking lot and waited for appropriate victims to pass by. He rejected black and hispanic customers and couldn't shoot the first white victim he saw because she had children with her. But when a white couple in their fifties came out of the store, they seemed perfect. Colwell shot both in the head, killing the husband first. He then drove to the local police station and calmly turned himself in.

Any murder is terrible, but to kill two people because you yourself want to die—and to do it in such a complicated and pointless fashion—well, it's like using a pair of hedge clippers to cut a coupon out of the newspaper, or brushing your hair one strand at a time, or kidnapping an entire high school wrestling team because you need help opening a jar of pickles, or—well, you get the point. It just doesn't make sense. But by the time he commited his capital crime, Colwell had made a habit out of doing nonsensical things.

Daniel Colwell was one of 14 children, raised in a home where hard work and deep faith were considered top priorities. Colwell was a good student who also excelled on the football field. But then everything changed while Colwell was in high school. The teenager started hearing strange voices.

One day he thought he saw the devil and the gates of hell appear in one of his classrooms. Colwell suddenly quit the football team and claimed that playing football was a sin.

Over the next few years, Colwell developed a love/hate relationship with religion. He moved to Louisiana to join the congregation of TV minister Jimmy Swaggart, but returned home dejected after Swaggart's highly-publicized prostitution scandal. Feeling like he had been duped by Christianity, Colwell began soliciting money from Donald Trump and other wealthy businessmen in order to fund an anti-religion campaign. When that didn't work, he stormed a local TV station armed with a toy gun and a kitchen knife and demanded that they put him on the air to spread his message of atheism—although he claimed to be acting under God's orders at the time.

Colwell eventually decided that death was the only escape from his troubled thoughts, so he hatched a plan to kidnap a prominent member of the community and, as a ransom demand, ask for drugs he could use to kill himself.

Once again, the metaphor of cutting coupons with a pair of hedge clippers comes to mind. Wouldn't shoplifting a few bottles of sleeping pills have been much easier?

Colwell's latest plan failed like all his previous ones, which eventually led to the double murder in the Wal-Mart parking lot. It looked like Colwell had finally achieved his goal, no matter how long and convuluted a path he had to follow to reach it.

As Colwell testified in court, it was obvious that he still hadn't decided how he felt about God and religion. At one point he said, "I'm God's personal psychiatrist. He tells me everything." He then claimed that God was bored of living and wanted to die. To help the big guy out, Colwell devised a complicated murder scheme. "I am going to pretend to become God's best friend," Colwell said. "I am going to ask God could I shave him with a razor. He is going to say yes. Then I am going to cut his throat."

Much to the chagrin of his lawyers, who were doing their best to save his life, Colwell campaigned tirelessly for a death sentence. "Me and Death are best friends, and we love each other," he told the courtroom during his trial. The gentle giant then gave a speech designed to keep any members of the jury from wavering on his punishment.

"Jurors, don't make something so simple so hard," he said. "I, Daniel Colwell, deserve the death penalty. If you release me, I will kill again. I am a monster and have no control over my instinct to kill. Look at me. I am smiling and show no anger. I am your next door neighbor, your grocery store clerk, but I will kill you."

His speech was so impassioned that it was hard to believe Colwell hadn't been hired by the prosecution team. He continued by saying "For those of you who might want to see me suffer by making me suffer for the rest of my life in prison, how do you know that I will not break out of prison and then torture your loved ones, such as your children, parents, or whoever you love deeply, even yourselves? Jurors, why take the risk? Why take that foolish risk? Again, why take the risk? Daniel Colwell must die!"

Apparently there were no risk takers on the jury, because Colwell was given the death sentence he so passionately requested. At the formal sentencing two days later, Colwell expressed his gratitude by standing up in court and serenading the crowd with the Styx song *Babe*.

Please take a moment to envision a 6-foot-tall, 300 pound convicted killer singing *Babe* to a crowded courtroom just after he's been sentenced to death. If you're like me, you're picturing those "I-just-wanted-to-be-on-TV" first-round rejections from *American Idol*—although no one from that show was ever executed for singing off-key or being "too pitchy."

Colwell's death sentence wasn't the end of the story, though. Before the state could carry out its punishment, Daniel Colwell opened the pickle jar all by himself by committing suicide in his cell. It's rumored that God has been visibly nervous ever since.

James Kelly Moss

Long before Colonel Sanders made his home state famous with his tasty chicken, the initials KFC probably had a different meaning; namely, Kentucky Fried Criminals. By the early 1960s, over a hundred inmates had already done a lap dance in the state's electric chair, which barely had time to cool down in-between executions. They finally gave Old Sparky a 35-year breather beginning in 1962, and the last man to sit there before that long hiatus has become a legend in the Kentucky legal system.

James "Kelly" Moss was 250 pounds of pure whoop ass. "He's what you'd call a psychopath," remarked one of the prosecuting attorneys in Kelly's trial. "Just a gorilla, a real brute of a man." Over six feet tall with flaming red hair, Moss was jailed nearly a dozen times for offenses ranging from assault to drunkenness.

Being locked up did nothing to curtail his horseplay. In prison, Moss would bang on his cell bars or set his mattress on fire just to get attention. He once kicked a police chief so hard that he broke the man's leg, and on another occasion he chased a cop with a butcher knife he'd managed to procure. His favorite playmates, though, were his fellow convicts; he liked to break their fingers and toes whenever he got bored.

Moss was 45 years old when he committed the crime that earned him the death penalty. His mother, Edna, had just married a 74-year-old retired railroad worker named Charles Abbitt. Abbitt was a scrappy little guy barely over five feet tall and less than half of Kelly's weight. He obviously didn't read up on step-parenting before marrying Edna, because he fought with Moss and his two brothers from the very start. In fact, friends said Abbitt liked to stand in the kitchen sharpening all the knives while loudly remarking that he would cut out his stepsons' hearts if they ever interfered with his marriage.

On the night of November 6, 1957, Moss showed up at his mother's house stinking like cheap booze and trying to bum cab fare. Edna wasn't home and apparently Charles Abbitt didn't feel like slipping his stepson the few bucks he was asking for. Abbitt ended up dead on the kitchen floor with eight broken ribs and a face so distorted even Picasso couldn't have dreamed it up. Someone had beaten him with a sink pipe and then slammed his head against the kitchen table, and the police could only think of one wild, red-haired hooligan who might be responsible.

The search for Kelly Moss began, and police found him the very next day—hiding in an outhouse behind an old Baptist church. He promptly blew his chances at denial by asking "How's the old man?" before authorities even started questioning him.

The trial was over before anybody could even blink. Moss wore a pink shirt in court—which somehow failed to make him appear more cute and cuddly—and testified on his own behalf, claiming that Abbitt attacked him and he had fought back in self-defense. An hour and a half later the jury returned with a guilty verdict, inciting Moss to scream profanity at the jurors. He had to be physically hauled out of the courtroom, and he even tried to tackle a cameraman who snapped his picture.

As the police were driving Moss to prison, he lunged over the back seat of the squad car and grabbed the steering wheel, causing the car to swerve off the road and into an alfalfa field. Moss decided to behave himself when he suddenly found several police revolvers tickling his scalp.

Although Kelly had already been sentenced to death, his case kept the local courts tied up in knots for years. First his execution date was postponed because Moss was in the middle of a divorce, then he later sued the state on the grounds that his guards were trying to kill him. Kelly had been using his cell bars as a makeshift xylophone one night and after he ignored repeated orders to pipe down, guards fired tear gas pellets into his cell. One of them hit Moss squarely in the ass, ripping a gash in one meaty cheek. Kelly picked at the scab constantly to keep the wound raw, then he would drop his pants in court to display the evidence of his mistreatment. His damaged rump obviously wasn't enough to sway the court, though, and his execution eventually proceeded as normal.

On his final day, Moss was scarfing down a last meal of steak, shrimp, and French fries when he received two unexpected visitors; his mother Edna and a local minister. Moss threw his dinner tray against the wall and screamed, "What are you doing here, you whore? If you hadn't married him in the first place, I wouldn't be in here!"

Edna hollered right back at her son while the minister launched into a sermon about the evils of capital punishment. Moss jumped up and started kicking the bars of his cell, howling like a caged yeti. He snarled at his mother, "You brought me into this mess, now goddammit, you can watch me go out of it!"

Prison officials dragged Edna to the warden's office and locked the minister in Kelly's cell. Dropping his fire and brimstone act, the minister hid in a corner as Moss continued to rant and rave.

Kelly was still in a foul mood when they led him to the electric chair at a few minutes past midnight. He grumbled to himself as the guards strapped him in and attached electrodes to his arms, legs, chest, and head. These had been dipped in salt water to prevent electrical burns, and a few drops of water trickled down into one of Kelly's slippers, throwing him into another tantrum. In fact, witnesses disagreed about the nature of his final words before the switch was thrown. They were either "I'm not guilty" or "Where's that damn water coming from?"

Edna remained locked in the warden's office for most of the night with a prison secretary to keep her company. The warden had unplugged the only clock in the room so Edna wouldn't throw a fit at the time of her son's execution, but when the ornery old lady noticed that the clock's hands weren't moving, she threw the fit anyway and stomped on the secretary's foot, breaking her toe.

Kelly was pronounced dead at 1:14 a.m., but the Moss legacy didn't end there. For years after the execution, the prosecutor who handled the case received dozens of threatening letters from Edna, which were always scribbled on toilet paper. James Kelly Moss may have been pushing up daisies, but his mother made sure there was still one member of the family out there raising hell.

Spotlight On: Jailhouse Jokers

You might assume that a death sentence would "kill" a person's sense of humor, but that's not always the case. Some death row inmates still laugh and kid around like they're in a college dorm instead of a maximum security cell block.

Keith Daniel Williams, convicted of a triple murder, once made a fake mouse out of a lint ball and broom straws then stuffed it down another death row inmate's pants. The other inmate felt the straws poking him and thought the mouse had bitten him, so he yanked off his pants and boxer shorts in front of a civilian group that was touring the prison facilities at the time. That inmate later retaliated by rubbing jalapeno juice on the end of a tube of hemorrhoid cream belonging to Williams.

Convicted killer Lesley Lee Gosch managed to turn a personal handicap into an opportunity for humor.

Gosch lost an eye during a failed science experiment as a teenager, and he wore a glass eye to disguise the infirmity. One day while he was in prison, Gosch took out his fake eye and dropped it among the cooked carrots on his dinner tray. He then called the guard who delivered the meal to his cell and told him, "Look, I want another tray. I don't know where the rest of him is, but I ain't eating this part."

Identical twins Carey and David Moore once pulled the kind of prank normally reserved for Disney films starring precocious child actors. Both men happened to be in the same prison at the same time, with Carey living on death row after a double murder conviction while David was serving a short term for theft. The Moores asked to have a private meeting to discuss family matters, and during the meeting the brothers exchanged clothes. Afterwards, Carey went to the prison kitchen to work his brother's scheduled shift while David sat calmly in Carey's death row cell. The ruse was discovered after a few hours, and the brothers were returned to their rightful places.

Ironically, the death row inmate who tried to generate the biggest laugh ended up being the biggest flop. During his long years in prison, double murderer Patrick Knight came up with an idea; he would ask people to send him jokes, then he would pick the best one and include it in his last words. The impromptu contest, which became known as "Dead Man Laughing," was organized using a web site set up by one of Knight's non-incarcerated friends.

"A little bit of levity is needed," Knight said when asked about the contest. "I just want to go out laughing. I'm not trying to disrespect anyone. I know I'm not innocent." The contest gained plenty of local publicity and Knight received nearly 1300 submissions, many of which dealt with capital punishment or the legal system. "Lawyer jokes are real popular," Knight said. "I'm not going to use any profanity if I can find the one I want, or any vulgar content. It wouldn't be bad if it was a little bit on the edge. That would be cool."

Knight and his fellow death row inmates planned to pick the winning entry. But when his execution date arrived and it was time for Knight to deliver his well-advertised rib-tickler, the condemned man apparently lost his nerve. "I said I was going to tell a joke," Knight began once he was strapped to the lethal injection table. "Death has set me free. That's the biggest joke. I deserve this." With his voice wavering, Knight then added, "And the other joke is that I am not Patrick Bryan Knight and y'all can't stop this execution now. Go ahead. I'm finished."

Knight's "joke" turned out to be more confusing than amusing. "It puzzled me a little bit," remarked a local law enforcement officer. "It wasn't much of a joke." A prison spokeswoman also disputed Knight's claim that he was really an imposter. "We fingerprint them when they come over," she explained.

Horace Kelly

Sanity's a funny thing, and sometimes it's hard to figure out who's crazier—the people who make the law, the people who break the law, or the people who interpret the law. If you need an example of this psycho-legal conundrum, look no further than the case of Horace Kelly.

Kelly was working as a security guard at a construction site in sunny California when one day he apparently snapped, killing three people in the span of six days. His first victim was a 25-year-old female hitchhiker. Kelly attempted to rape her then shot her twice, killing her. He repeated the offense the following day, this time with a 43-year-old woman who Kelly saw walking down the street as he was driving home. Again, the victim was both raped and killed, although the sexual assault continued after the woman was dead.

The following week, Kelly attempted to abduct a 13-year-old girl who was walking home from a convenience store with her 11-year-old male cousin. The boy kicked Kelly in the shins, allowing the girl to run away. Kelly shot the boy twice, killing him. Kelly was arrested that night with the murder weapon still in his possession. He claimed innocence at first, then confessed to his crimes when the 13-year-old girl identified him in a lineup. Kelly was charged and convicted on three counts of murder and one count of attempted murder, and was given the death penalty.

But 13 years later, as Kelly's execution date loomed, the state called a hearing to determine if he was mentally competent enough to be executed. Under California law, a prisoner who becomes insane while in prison can't be executed, even if he was deemed sane during his trial. If the prisoner no longer understands the nature of his crime or of his impending capital punishment, the execution must be delayed until the prisoner's mental condition improves.

It's easy to see why the competency hearing was arranged. During his 13 years in prison, Horace Kelly had developed some pretty bizarre tendencies. Prison officials reported that Kelly spent most of his time crouching in his cell or sitting on the edge of his cot with a blank stare on his face, sometimes wearing nothing but bed sheets and a turban. He rarely spoke, and when he did he only muttered under his breath or spouted a hodge-podge of numbers, legal terms, and bureaucratic slang that one psychiatrist dubbed "incoherent word salad."

For example, when Kelly was asked about the crimes he had committed, he responded with:

"I'm here to go to college because of courtroom unusual projects, because of hospitals. I am on delayed punishment. Throw the book at me, correct it later. Another CC then 00."

When Kelly was asked if he had ever killed anyone, he said:

"As testament of names, verses."

When that same question was repeated, Kelly said:

"Two years and a month."

When asked if he knew the significance of his execution date, Kelly said:

"Superman, spy man numbers."

When asked how he felt about his upcoming execution, Kelly said:

"Over property, against family, versus other families to do with education."

The psychiatric evaluations seemed to confirm what prison officials had claimed all along; that Kelly had no idea who he was, where he was, or why he was there in the first place. Kelly seemed to think that prison was actually a vocational school, and that when his time was up he would be getting a diploma rather than getting executed. He thought the courtroom proceedings were being held to clear up some insurance matters, and that the judge's job was to decide if Kelly could enlist in the Marines.

But while Horace Kelly's perceptions were disturbing, his increased lack of personal hygiene had become flat-out intolerable. "Smelly Kelly," as he was known by prison staff, rarely showered, changed his clothes, or flushed his toilet. He hoarded food in his cell until it rotted, then refused to throw it away. Kelly also used his own feces to finger-paint on his cell walls, and he once mixed his bodily waste with hair and egg yolks, rolled it into a ball, then displayed the result proudly like some hellish art class project. Prison staff were forced to wear masks and gloves when they hosed out his cell or escorted Kelly to psychiatric evaluations or court hearings.

One would think that finding Horace Kelly insane would be a slam-dunk for any defense lawyer, but such was not the case; after the competency hearing, Kelly was deemed sane enough to execute. Although six out of seven mental health experts said Kelly was out of his mind, the seventh thought he was perfectly fine. Her criteria? She claimed that Kelly was able to name his favorite basketball team, he correctly read the ingredient list from a soda can, and he had beaten her twice at tic-tac-toe.

There were a few things that bothered her, though, like the fact that when Kelly was asked to draw a person, his picture looked more like a desk lamp. Kelly had also seen his dead father wandering around the courtroom. "They have look-alikes here," he explained. When Kelly was asked at one point if he was concerned about his execution, he said no. "I've had numerous executions in the past, and they haven't done me any harm."

Despite the controversy, the court declared that Horace Kelly could be given a new execution date—but to this day, he hasn't. He now spends most of his time watching TV in his cell. And while he never complains and hasn't caused trouble in years, the guards still have to remind "Smelly Kelly" to take a shower every once in a while.

Christopher Newton

How can you tell when an execution is taking way too long to complete? When the condemned man has to ask for a bathroom break in the middle of it. It sounds bizarre, but that's just one of the curious aspects of Christopher Newton's life and death.

Newton spent most of his early years in trouble. The high school dropout was arrested multiple times for offenses that ranged from shoplifting candy bars to grand theft. Despite his good sense of humor and his reputation as the "class clown," Newton also had an unhealthy interest in Satanism and a habit of performing questionable acts, such as inappropriate sexual behavior and setting his family's house on fire.

After being released from prison following a 7-year sentence for burglary, Newton had a hard time adjusting to the outside world. A few weeks later

Newton burglarized his own father's house, purposefully leaving behind plenty of fingerprints. Newton was convicted and sentenced to another 8-to-15-year prison term, achieving his goal of getting back to the one place he felt safe and comfortable. But once he was back in prison, Newton apparently changed his mind.

"You don't want to spend your life in a hell hole," he once remarked. "Nothing against the prison system, but it's not the funnest place to be."

Newton decided that since he didn't want to live in prison and couldn't live outside of prison, he didn't want to live at all. Through a series of lies and manipulations, the 6-foot, 225-lb convict arranged to share a cell with Jason Brewer, a man only half his size. Newton then waited for his new cellmate to aggravate him so that Newton would have an excuse to kill him.

It wasn't long before Newton got his wish. After an argument over a game of chess, the big convict flew into a violent rage.

"He kept giving up," Newton later explained. "Every time I put him in check, he'd give up and want to start a new game. And I tried to tell him you never give up. You never know when your opponent is going to make a mistake, so you play it out until you can't play it out any more. I just got tired of it."

In a rather drastic version of "checkmate," Newton punched, kicked, and stomped Brewer, then slammed the other man's head against the floor. When Brewer didn't seem to be bleeding enough, Newton stomped him some more. He then strangled the other man with a strip of cloth torn from his prison jumpsuit.

When correctional officers rushed to the cell, they found a smiling Newton sitting there calmly with blood smeared on his face. "Welcome to the house of death!" he exclaimed. As paramedics tried to revive Brewer, Newton laughed and said, "Let him die. I killed him. Fuck that bitch. You might as well not even work on him. He's already dead." Newton then began singing a made-up song that included the lyrics, "There's nothing like the taste of fresh blood in the morning."

Brewer was later declared dead, and Newton received the death penalty for the murder—which was fine with him. He gave a full confession of his crime and never fought his new sentence. "I'm a Republican on death row," he said. "I'm for the death penalty. If you're sentenced to it, they should carry it out."

As years passed by, Newton awaited his fate with gleeful anticipation. On the one-year anniversary of Brewer's murder, Newton made paper hats and party favors and invited the prison psychiatrist to celebrate the festive occasion with him.

When Brewer's execution day arrived, he consumed a last meal of two T-bone steaks, asparagus, Brussels sprouts, feta cheese, rye bread with butter, watermelon, German chocolate cake, and cream soda. The condemned man seemed calm, relaxed, and ready to meet his fate. But when Newton—who had somehow grown to a whopping 265 pounds on a diet of prison food—arrived at the lethal injection chamber, the problems began.

Execution technicians tried to find insertion points for the needles in both of Newton's arms, but came up empty. "He was thick, and his veins sat deep," remarked one prison official. They then tried his elbows, wrists, hands, and right leg, sticking Newton nearly a dozen times in the process. At one point, a prison spokeswoman held up a note to witnesses in the viewing chamber that said *We have told the team to take their time. His size is creating a problem.*

After an hour had passed, Newton asked for a bathroom break and the request was granted. He was escorted back to the chamber a few minutes later, and the process began again. Newton didn't seem bothered by the long delay, and even laughed and joked with the technicians during the procedure.

Ninety minutes after the process began, Newton was finally moved from the medical chamber to the adjoining death chamber. When asked if he had any last words, Newton replied, "Boy, I could sure go for some beef stew and a chicken bone. That's it."

The lethal drugs began to flow, and Newton was declared dead 16 minutes later. Prison officials expressed concern because the drugs normally do their work in less than eight minutes. But the one person without a care in the world was Christopher Newton, who finally got everything he wanted—with the exception of that chicken bone.

Charles Singleton

When convenience store owner Mary Lou York was killed, no CSI crew was needed. No detective with Sherlock Holmes skills was summoned. There was no need to search for fingerprints or study security camera footage. From a law enforcement standpoint, solving the crime was a no-brainer.

Charles Singleton, a teenage boy who knew York, walked into the store one summer night and asked for a pack of cigarettes. He then pulled out a gun and demanded all the money from the cash register. York resisted and Singleton fired his gun, but missed. He then pulled out a knife and stabbed York twice in the neck.

A customer was in the store at the time, and she happened to be a relative of Singleton's who had seen him enter. As York was stabbed, the store owner called out "Go get help! Charles Singleton is killing me!" The customer ran to fetch the police, and Singleton ran away as well. He was seen leaving the store by yet another customer. When police arrived, York identified Singleton as her attacker before she died.

Considering the evidence, there was no way for Singleton to escape from justice. He was arrested, convicted, and given the death penalty. But after a few years in prison, Singleton—who had lived a mostly normal life until that point—began to see things a bit differently. His mindset became a curious mix of religious zeal, science fiction, and elements from both horror movies and action flicks.

Singleton sometimes referred to himself as God, or the Holy Spirit, or "God and the Supreme Court." At other times he said he was only a marionette whose strings were being pulled by God. He added that he and his sidekick St. John had been sent on a holy mission; to rid the world of homosexuals. Singleton also claimed that he had received divine orders to kill both his prison psychiatrist and the President of the United States.

Believe it or not, those are some of the most lucid things Singleton said while in prison. He also announced that his cell had demons in it, and complained about the mess they had made with their "demon blood." Because of a "voodoo curse," Singleton's food sometimes changed into worms and his cigarettes changed into bones. He was also convinced that prison doctors had implanted a thought-stealing device behind his right ear, which was activated every time he read the Bible. The entire staff was also using "subliminal suggestions" on him, which Singleton tried his best to ignore. He wasn't worried, though, because Sylvester Stallone and Arnold Schwarzenegger were on their way to save him—as soon as they escaped from a parallel universe, that is.

There was little doubt that Singleton's mental state had deteriorated while he was locked up. Prison staff reported him as being "nude and zombie-like" much of the time. Singleton also stopped eating at one point, and he once tore his mattress into tiny pieces and flushed it down the toilet. He was deemed a possible danger to both himself and others in the prison. Medication made Singleton far more manageable, but there was one problem with the scenario; as long as he took it, he would be deemed mentally fit to die when his execution date rolled around.

Singleton himself wasn't overly concerned about his date with death. He claimed that he had tried suicide once by cutting his own throat, but that the bleeding had miraculously stopped. He also believed that the execution process would only stop his breathing temporarily, and that a judge could restart his breathing at a later time. He also wondered why he was being executed at all since his victim was still alive. "She is somewhere on this earth waiting for me, her groom," Singleton once wrote in a letter to court officials. "Somebody sent me, the robot, to Mrs. York. I know the police is in it. You could be in it. So, if her service was/is in vain, it's because that's the way you want it."

The issue of whether or not to medicate Singleton became a heated debate in both the media and the judicial world. Some judges cited an earlier Supreme Court ruling that made it illegal to execute an insane prisoner, and said that medicating Singleton was just a way to keep him mentally sound until the state killed him. But the majority of judges said that the overall benefits of the drugs were the most important factor. While taking them, Singleton would remain calm and stable during his time in prison. One judge wrote, "Eligibility for execution is the only unwanted consequence of the medication."

Sort of makes the side effects of those other popular drugs—dry mouth, headaches, constipation, etc—pale by comparison, doesn't it?

In the end, Singleton did continue taking the medication—and he was executed. Beforehand, he enjoyed a last meal of two soybean burgers, fried eggplant, fried green tomatoes, fried sweet potato slices, baked beans, potato salad, doughnuts, and two vanilla milkshakes.

Instead of speaking his last words, Singleton wrote a long letter which was read aloud after his death. Part of it stated, "The blind think I'm playing a game. They deny me, refusing me existence. But everybody takes the place of another. You have taught me what you want done— and I will not let you down."

Singleton was put to death on January 6, 2004—and contrary to the plotline of most action flicks, Stallone and Schwarzenegger didn't burst into the execution chamber at the very last minute to stop the lethal injection.

Spotlight On: Laughable Lawsuits

What do you get when you combine too much free time with a generous amount of state-funded legal aid? A lot of pointless, trivial, and often bizarre lawsuits. Death row inmates who get tired of staring at the walls or planning their last meal menu have found endless ways to irritate local lawmakers by filing lawsuits that typically do nothing but waste taxpayer money.

A few of the lawsuits do have merit on the surface. The state of Ohio has been snarled in legal red tape for years due to a lack of confidence in its execution protocol. Ohio switched from a 3-drug "cocktail" to a single-dose recipe for its lethal injections, and several executions have been botched or delayed as a result. One inmate even complained, "This isn't working!" as he lay strapped to the lethal injection table.

Roy Willard Blankenship, executed in Georgia, also took legal action regarding his lethal injection drugs. In his case, he claimed that the state's supply of sodium thiopental—a sedative used in the execution process—had expired, and might therefore be harmful to his health.

One has to wonder about lawsuits such as this one; after all, that ancient container of yogurt in the back of the fridge probably won't kill you, but those lethal injection drugs were designed to do just that—which would make them defective if they *weren't* harmful to your health.

Back in lawsuit-plagued Ohio, another lengthy legal battle involves an inmate who demanded meals prepared in the Halal style so he could remain faithful to the tenants of the Islamic religion. Simply banning pork products wouldn't be enough; any animals fed to the Islamic inmates would also have to be slaughtered and prepared in the very strict style dictated by the religion. Ohio is worried that feeding thousands of self-declared Islamic prisoners in this fashion would bankrupt the state, while airline passengers—most of whom no longer get any food at all, not even the meager "beef or chicken" option from years past—wonder what they would have to do to warrant such special treatment.

While some inmates worry about feeding their souls, others worry about feeding their libidos. Robert Gattis, a Delaware inmate whose death sentence was commuted to life without parole, sued the state on the basis that denying him pornographic magazines violated his constitutional rights. Death row inmate Gary Bradford Cone took similar actions against the state of Tennessee when they implemented a ban against sexually-explicit materials.

An item doesn't need to be racy or provocative to prompt a lawsuit. Donald Edward Beaty tried to sue the state of Arizona when officials wouldn't allow him to play his Nintendo Game Boy while on death row. Kevin Singer, currently serving life in prison for murder, filed suit against Wisconsin when the state decided to ban all *Dungeons & Dragons* gaming materials from the prison system. Officials claimed the game might foster violent tendencies, gang-like behavior, and escape-related fantasies.

Some lawsuits add insult to injury, but the one filed by death row resident William Deparvine added insult to homicide. Deparvine, convicted of murdering a married couple after meeting with them on the pretense of buying their vintage Chevy truck, filed a lawsuit from death row to gain possession of the aforementioned vehicle. Using a phony bill of sale with forged signatures as evidence, Deparvine hoped to be given ownership of the truck—despite the fact that driving it would never be an option.

When it comes to bizarre prison lawsuits, though, the state of California definitely takes the cake. Serial killer Randy Kraft, who was convicted of the sexual torture murders of 16 men—including one who was found dead in Kraft's car when police arrested him—once sued an author who wrote a book about Kraft's crimes. Kraft claimed that the author portrayed him as being "without moral values," and that the book would seriously hurt Kraft's chances of future employment if he was ever released from prison. Some business experts agreed, citing the fact that next to a lack of work experience and an incomplete job history, nothing tarnishes a résumé more than uncontrolled murderous rage.

But even Randy Kraft's legal high jinks pale in comparison with those of fellow California death row inmate Lawrence Bittaker. Bittaker was convicted on multiple counts of rape, murder, and kidnapping after he and an accomplice killed a string of teenage girls in 1979. The men used ice picks, pliers, sledgehammers, and other weapons during their assaults, some of which were recorded on audio tape so the men could relive the crimes afterward.

When the tape was played in court during Bittaker's trial, many people openly wept and some had to leave the courtroom before they got sick.

Imagine the irony, then, of Lawrence Bittaker filing a lawsuit against the state of California for "cruel and unusual punishment." What awful treatment could inspire such a vicious, hardened killer to sue his captors, you may ask? Well, I'll tell you.

Bittaker claimed that the cookies on his prison lunch trays were sometimes broken, and that from time to time the bread on his sandwiches was a little soggy. It's hard to image the anguish Bittaker must have felt whenever he saw a cracked Oreo or touched that spongy bread.

Seriously, I mean that. It *is* hard to imagine. Some might even label it *impossible* to imagine. But then again, I'm no lawyer. Perhaps the nuances of our legal system merely escape me.

Varnall Weeks

Some people look at a Jackson Pollock painting—those big canvases splattered with random drips and smears of paint—and wonder how a kindergarten kid's art project wound up hanging in a museum. Others fall to their knees in awe and praise Pollock as a pioneer in the Abstract Expressionist movement. In other words, genius is in the eye of the beholder.

Such was the case with Varnall Weeks, a convicted killer who was either brilliant or demented, depending on who you asked.

From the moment he committed his capital crime, Weeks displayed a flair for nonsensical words and actions. He killed a young veterinary student in Alabama and stole the man's Honda Civic, then drove the stolen car to Ohio. In Cleveland, Weeks was stopped by local police for making an illegal left turn. When asked for his license, Weeks gave police the one belonging to his murder victim. He then shot and wounded the police officer and tried to escape on foot, but another officer shot Weeks and he was eventually apprehended.

After his arrest, Weeks claimed innocence—despite the fact that he was driving the murder victim's car, had possession of the victim's driver's license, and was still carrying the gun used to commit the crime. Instead of admitting that he stole his victim's car, Weeks claimed that he had taken a bus from Alabama to Ohio in order to buy clothes—just like any normal person would. The tale Weeks spun of that multi-day journey included hookups with anonymous women, a marijuana-filled joyride with an anonymous man, and a fight with an anonymous opponent outside a McDonald's restaurant. Weeks claimed that he lost both his shoes and injured his foot during that battle, but just like his other stories, police found no evidence that it actually happened.

Hard evidence won out over imaginative storytelling and Weeks was eventually convicted of capital murder during a robbery, an offense worthy of the death penalty. It was during the sentencing phase that things really turned interesting. Weeks chose to let the judge, rather than the jury, decide his punishment, adding that he would prefer death.

Because of the odd behavior Weeks had shown while in custody—coupled with a history of mental instability—the judge decided to ask Weeks a series of questions to determine how mentally sound the man was.

On the first day of questioning, Weeks showed up in court wearing a homemade headband fashioned from a domino and a piece of string. The numbers on the domino were a double seven, and Weeks explained that the game piece represented him, because there were seven days in a week and his name was, coincidentally, Weeks. Believe it or not, that was probably the sanest act Weeks performed during the competency hearing.

As the judge questioned Weeks, the killer's answers ran the gamut from sane and sensible to Cuckoo for Cocoa Puffs. Weeks answered the first few questions accurately; he knew who he was and why he had been arrested and convicted. He also knew who his lawyer and the judge were, although Weeks said he was also a judge who could kill the other judge any time he felt like it.

When asked more complex questions, Weeks rambled on about his favorite topics such as the Garden of Eden, albinos, Aztecs, cybernetics, and his love of rainy weather. Weeks also claimed to be God, and said he wasn't afraid to die because after his execution he would be reincarnated as a giant turtle who would then rule the universe.

Instead of being flabbergasted, the judge actually seemed entranced by the killer's odd ideas. A portion of the court transcripts are provided below:

VARNALL WEEKS: Well, as creation is desired, you got the adults and you got the children. You've got two adults, and you've got a child. And you've got a man on one side and a woman on the other side, and you've got the child which would be the one in the center. Okay?

But as creation is concerned, it is the child that causes the parents to come together. You see? I haven't—the child is causing the parents to create, you know, the child. Well, in the creation of God, it works the same way. The parents—the child is the creator of the parents, but the parents is to bring forth the child, you see.

JUDGE: Can you tell me how the word "rifle" or "gun" or "weapon" would be—can you show me how they would relate to what you just said?

VARNALL WEEKS: Well, in the military we call it a weapon. The—no, I think it's the other way around. I think it's a weapon in the court of law. It's a weapon—but in the military it's a firearm—or either I may have it crossed up. Either—either one way or the other—a gun, well, that's ghetto slang. You know, that's more or less slang or something of that nature, so it's not really recognized as—it has no honorable respect using that term, like "nigger," you know. It's offensive. See what I'm saying?

JUDGE: I understand exactly what you're saying.

I can think of several appropriate responses to the speech Varnall Weeks gave, including "Could you repeat that, please, but with slightly less batshit craziness?" or "My goodness. People from your planet certainly have interesting theories." But the judge's response—"I understand exactly what you're saying"—seems almost as nutty as what Weeks said.

While the psychologists who examined Weeks used terms like "paranoid schizophrenic" and "delusional," the judge tossed out glowing phrases like "remarkable," "highly intelligent," and "shows signs of genius."

The judge explained his admiration for Weeks's philosophy by saying, "It's not so much as what's being said, but what is being meant." He also admitted that Weeks did fit the dictionary definition of insanity, and that Weeks was "what the average person on the street would regard to be insane."

Weeks was executed in Alabama's electric chair on May 12, 1995. So far, astronomers have seen no signs of a giant turtle hovering in Earth's atmosphere—but they're keeping an eye out just in case.

Aileen Wuornos

Some killers never admit to their crimes. Other boast about them. Some claim insanity while others swear to be mentally sound. Some accept their punishment calmly. Others kick, scream, and curse at the judge and jury as they're sentenced.

And then you have Aileen Wuornos—one of the most colorful people to ever occupy death row—who did all of the above.

Aileen's life of crime began at age 18 when she was jailed and charged with drunk driving, disorderly conduct, and firing a weapon from a moving vehicle. Wuornos skipped town to avoid her court date and eventually hitchhiked all the way from Michigan to Florida. Soon after her arrival in the Sunshine State, she met and married a wealthy 69-year-old yacht club president. The marriage ended after only nine weeks, though, because Wuornos was constantly getting into bar fights and beating her elderly husband with his walking cane—behavior which raised quite a few eyebrows during those prim and proper yacht club events.

Wuornos returned to Michigan, then spent nearly a decade drifting around the country and causing trouble. She was arrested at one point for throwing a pool ball at a bartender and hitting him in the head. She later robbed a convenience store, scoring $35 and two packs of cigarettes in the hold-up. Over the next few months she wrote forged checks, stole weapons and ammunition, attacked a man with a beer bottle, and attempted other armed robberies. She was also cited for such mundane offenses as speeding, driving without a valid license, and, as one landlord claimed, "painting the walls dark brown without his permission." A remark written on one of the citations said, "Attitude poor. Thinks she is above the law."

Despite the fact that Wuornos could barely step outside her apartment without doing something illegal, police were slow to link all the crimes together since she used several different aliases and multiple sets of ID. By 1989, though, her behavior had become so wild and erratic that she seemed to have a permanent home on police radar. She got into brawls with bus drivers, committed acts of vandalism, and once spent six days making threatening calls to a supermarket because of a disagreement over lottery tickets. Wuornos also started carrying a gun in her purse and went out of her way to pick fights with anyone she met.

Wuornos committed her first murder at the end of that year. She had worked off and on as a prostitute for most of her adult life, and in November of 1989 she accepted a ride from an electronics shop owner who stopped and asked if she was available. Wuornos shot the man three times, dumped his body in the woods, and stole his car. She later claimed that the man tried to rape her and that the shooting was in self-defense, but the truth was never known since Wuornos changed her story so many times.

Over the next year, Wuornos shot and killed six more men. As the body count grew, police realized they had a serial killer on their hands. By analyzing fingerprints found in the victims' cars and on stolen items pawned after the killings, investigators at the National Crime Information Center were finally able to link Wuornos to her assorted aliases. A manhunt began and Wuornos was found in Port Orange, Florida, but police chose to track her movements instead of arresting her because they suspected her female lover might be involved in the crimes as well.

Police then used a clever ploy; they arrested Wuornos for some of her minor charges and, while she was safely in jail, interrogated her female lover for information. Wuornos eventually confessed to six of the murders, but insisted that her lover had no involvement and that all six men had tried to assault her before they were killed in self-defense—although her story sometimes changed. At one point, she claimed that none of the men had assaulted her and she only killed them out of fear that they would. When her lawyer scolded her for making comments like that to the police, Wuornos replied, "They want to hang me...and that's cool, because maybe, man, I deserve it."

After her arrest, Wuornos became a media starlet. She was dubbed the first female serial killer in America because her crimes fit a very distinct pattern established by the FBI; she had killed more than three people, the victims were all strangers with no connection to each other, and time had passed between each murder. Wuornos was glorified by those who believed her claims of self-defense and vilified by those who focused on her title as the "Damsel of Death." Books and movies about Wuornos were quickly released, and a composer in California even produced an opera based on her life.

The circus atmosphere surrounding the case increased when the trail began. Her defense team wanted Wuornos to plead guilty in exchange for a life sentence, but prosecutors refused to make a deal and sought the death penalty based on overwhelming evidence related to the first murder. During the trial, jurors were unconvinced by the self-defense claim and seemed put off by Wuornos' demeanor and the fact that she continually pled the Fifth Amendment while under oath—a tactic which practically screams "guilty" in most cases.

And guilty is what the jury found her, after less than two hours of deliberation. Wuornos responded by screaming at the jurors, "I'm innocent! I was raped! I hope you get raped! Scumbags of America!" It was no surprise when a death sentence was handed down shortly thereafter.

Over the next few months, Wuornos see-sawed back and forth between claims of guilt and innocence—and her courtroom manners fluctuated as well. Wuornos claimed no contest to five additional murder charges, but no charges were filed for her seventh victim because the body was never found. She appeared to accept her fate gracefully, saying that she wouldn't fight the other murder charges because she wanted to "get right with God," but as the judge piled more death sentences on top of the one she already had, Wuornos flipped him off and hissed "Motherfucker!" She told the assistant state attorney, "I hope your wife and children get raped in the ass!"

After the trial, Wuornos proclaimed her innocence. "Everything they said about me was so full of lying," she said. "It wasn't funny. None of that stuff was true." But as time passed by, she changed her tune. In a later interview, she said "I've got to come clean that I killed those seven men in first-degree murder and robbery. There was no self-defense. I'm being straight-up about everything." When asked about the rape and assault claims, she replied, "That was just my lying gig, trying to beat the system."

Although automatic appeals are filed in every death penalty case, Wuornos instructed her lawyers to drop all of hers. She admitted her guilt and was ready and willing to accept her punishment. "I killed those men, robbed them as cold as ice, and I'd do it again, too. I have hate crawling through my system. I'm one who seriously hates human life and would kill again."

Wuornos also hated the living conditions in prison. She complained that the prison workers were mistreating her, her mattress wasn't comfortable, and the water pressure in her cell was too low. She also accused her keepers of trying to drive her crazy. "They were using sonic pressure on me," she said. "It was crushing my head. And I think they had some kind of an eye in the cell."

Ironically, the fact that Wuornos accepted her sentence caused the courts to question her sanity. They ordered a series of mental evaluations, which Wuornos wasn't happy about. In one interview she said, "United States Supreme Court, you fucking— I'm telling you, man, you mother fuckers keep fucking with my goddamn execution, there's gonna be bloodshed. I'm sick of this."

The tests concluded that Wuornos was cognizant, lucid, and totally sane. "She knew exactly what she was doing," said the state attorney, who witnessed one of the exams. "She's pretty bright, very quick, and very deliberate."

Wuornos seemed calmly optimistic as her execution date drew near. She spoke frequently about God and religion—but instead of the King James Bible, she must have been reading the King James T. Kirk Bible, because her version of the gospel was heavily-laced with science fiction.

Death Row's Oddest Inmates

Regarding her execution, Wuornos said, "God is going to be there, Jesus Christ is going to be there, all the angels and everything. I think it's going to be more like Star Trek, beaming me up into a space vehicle, man. Then I move on, recolonize to another planet or whatever."

On October 9, 2002, Wuornos was brought to the death chamber—or teleportation pad, depending on your religious affiliation. She had refused a last meal, drinking only a cup of coffee prior to her lethal injection. When asked if she had any last words, she said, "Yes. I'd just like to say I'm sailing with the Rock and I'll be back like Independence Day, with Jesus, June 6th. Like the movie, big mother ship and all. I'll be back."

No one knows if "the Rock" refers to Jesus (Psalm 18:2, "The Lord is my rock.") or actor/wrestler Dwayne "The Rock" Johnson. But if Aileen Wuornos really is flying around in a starship with either one of them, let's hope they don't run into that giant turtle that used to be Varnall Weeks. It could start a space battle that would make the most outrageous Japanese monster movie look tame by comparison.

Spotlight On: Massive Last Meals

The last meal tradition has always been one of the most fascinating aspects of the execution process. Most states allow their condemned inmates to choose anything they want—within certain limits—with the exception of Maryland and Texas. States like California and Florida offer a generous spending limit while others put a price cap of 10 to 20 dollars on the food for the final meal. Some states also allow fast food or restaurant take-out while others only serve items available in the prison kitchen at the time.

Every possible variety of last meal has been served throughout the years. There have been large meals and small meals, sweet meals and salty meals, healthy meals and gluttonous meals. Prisoners have ordered Italian, Chinese, Mexican, and a variety of other ethnic cuisines in addition to good old-fashioned American favorites. Some have gone heavy on the vegetables, others gorge on fresh fruit. A few have ordered nothing but huge portions of meat. Some had dessert only. Some asked for nothing but a beverage. Others asked for nothing at all.

But in Texas—where everything is bigger—a contest to consume the largest last meal seemed to be going on for years. Before a recent change in policy, some inmates were ordering enough food to feed an entire family. These lists of last meal menus (although not all requests were granted) show that Texas prisoners never lose their appetite, even when death is mere hours away.

David Castillo asked for 24 tacos, six enchiladas, six tostadas, two cheeseburgers, two whole onions, five jalapeno peppers, a chocolate milkshake, and a quart of milk.

Stanley Allison Baker Jr. requested two 16 oz. rib eye steaks, one pound of thinly-sliced turkey breast, 12 strips of bacon, two large hamburgers with mayo, onion, and lettuce, two large baked potatoes with butter, sour cream, cheese, and chives, four slices of cheese or one-half pound of grated cheddar cheese, chef salad with bleu cheese dressing, two ears of corn on the cob, one pint of mint chocolate chip ice cream, and four cans of vanilla Coke or Mr. Pibb.

Peter Miniel ordered 20 beef tacos, 20 beef enchiladas, two double cheeseburgers, a pizza with jalapenos, fried chicken, spaghetti, half of a chocolate cake, half of a vanilla cake, cookies and cream ice cream, caramel pecan fudge ice cream, a small fruit cake, two Cokes, two Pepsis, two root beers, and two glasses of orange juice.

Karl Chamberlain asked for one bacon double cheeseburger, two pieces of fried chicken, one bean and cheese quesadilla, a three-egg omelet with ham, mushrooms, onions, and cheese, two barbecue pork rolls, a half-pound of French fries covered with cheese, salsa, and jalapenos, onion rings, a chef salad, slices of cheese and lunchmeat, two deviled eggs, six fried jalapenos stuffed with cheese, a fresh vegetable tray, a fresh fruit tray, a pitcher of orange juice, and a pitcher of milk.

Jesse Mott ate two pounds of sirloin steak, two pounds of cured ham, 12 fried eggs, 50 biscuits, two quarts of ice cream, two chocolate pies, and a gallon of lemonade.

In 2011, however, Texas put an end to such extravagant meals. The straw that broke the camel's back—or rather, the meal that broke the back of the person who had to carry it—belonged to Lawrence

Death Row's Oddest Inmates

Brewer. He ordered two chicken fried steaks smothered in gravy with sliced onions, a triple meat bacon cheeseburger with fixings on the side, a cheese omelet with ground beef, tomatoes, onions, bell peppers, and jalapenos, a large bowl of fried okra with ketchup, one pound of barbecue with half a loaf of white bread, three fajitas with fixings, a meat lovers pizza, three root beers, one pint of Blue Bell vanilla ice cream, and a slab of peanut butter fudge with crushed peanuts.

But it wasn't the massive amount of food that ticked off Texas lawmakers—it was the fact that Brewer refused to eat even a single bite of his meal. After the feast was hauled to his cell, Brewer turned up his nose and said he wasn't really hungry. That infuriated Senator John Whitmire, chairman of the Senate Criminal Justice Committee, who then wrote to the head of the Texas Department of Criminal Justice and recommended that Texas inmates no longer be allowed to order special last meals. The Texas officials agreed, and now Texas death row inmates are served the same meal as every other prisoner, even on the day of their execution.

Just like Davy Crockett and Pecos Bill, those huge last meals are now merely the stuff of legend in the Lone Star State. And on moonlit nights, when a restless wind stirs the trees on the Texas plains and coyotes howl in the distance, the convicts on death row whisper tall tales about T-bone steaks as big as a man and chocolate pies so sweet they'd bring a tear to the eye of the most ruthless criminal.

Stanley Baker Jr.

The award-winning children's book *Because of Winn-Dixie* is about a lonely girl whose life changes forever after she adopts a stray dog—but it could have just as easily been about a Texas man born in France who robs an adult video store and kills the clerk before embarking on a nationwide murder spree.

I'll admit, the first plot has far more commercial appeal.

Stanley Baker Jr. was born in Paris, where his father was stationed while serving in the Army. The family then moved to San Antonio, Texas, where Baker grew up. He spent four years in the Army himself, then joined the National Guard and started taking college classes with the goal of becoming a history teacher. That calm, respectable career path got derailed, though—because of Winn-Dixie.

Baker had been working as a stock clerk for the grocery store chain for several years when his boss suddenly switched Baker from the day shift to the night shift. Baker went ballistic and decided to quit, sending his boss an angry resignation letter. "Though I've given four years to your store, I've long felt my efforts were unappreciated," Baker wrote.

But apparently the letter wasn't enough to purge Baker's bad feelings. The former stock clerk put on green fatigues, grabbed a 12-gauge shotgun, and began walking to the grocery store with the intent to kill his former boss and anyone else who was in the store at the time. After plodding along for two miles, though, Baker got hot and tired, so he did what anyone in that situation would do—he entered an adult video store and decided to rob it.

Wayne John Walters, who ran the cash register at Dolar Video, was the only person in the store at the time. Baker raised his gun and demanded all the money plus the keys to Walters's truck. Walters complied immediately, but Baker shot him three times anyway. As the last shot was fired, the shotgun recoiled and smacked Baker in the face, splitting his lip and chipping a tooth.

Embarrassed about committing mass murder with blood on his face and a less-than-perfect smile, Baker abandoned his plan to kill everyone at the Winn-Dixie. Instead, he drove the stolen truck to his home, loaded up his belongings, and headed out of town. He had barely driven 70 miles when he was stopped and arrested by state troopers.

Inside the truck, police found a variety of weapons, ammunition, and survival gear. They also found a notebook with Baker's "to-do" list written in it, but instead of tasks like *pick up milk* and *water the plants*, the list included things such as *30+ victims dead*, *30+ armed robberies*, and *steal a lot of cars*. Baker also wrote about his hatred for gays, blacks, and President Clinton, and he had come up with detailed plans for a murder spree. A map of New York City had the words *the ultimate hunting ground* written on it.

Baker was tried, convicted, and given a death sentence for his crime. During a death row interview, he said he wasn't really sure what prompted the deadly incident. "It's weird the way it happened," he remarked. "It's like I went insane." And while his attorneys tried to get his death sentence overturned, Baker accepted his fate with calm resignation. "I'm looking forward to the last meal, but not the part that comes after it," he joked.

After eight years of prison food, Baker was obviously hungry for some real chow. For his last meal he ordered a huge feast that included two rib eye steaks, two hamburgers, two baked potatoes, four soft drinks, and ice cream for dessert.

Prison officials promised to do their best with Baker's meal order, but at that time special meal requests could only be honored if the food was available in the prison kitchen. A prison spokesman said they might have a tough time coming up with the steaks, but he did promise that Baker would be served meat "from a cow."

On the day of his execution, Baker was asked if he had any last words. He shrugged and said "Well, I don't have anything to say, so let's go." The warden asked if he was sure about that, and Baker replied, "I'm just sorry about what I did to Mr. Peters, that's all."

That apology might have been meaningful—except for the fact that the victim's last name was Walters.

Edwin Hart Turner

Considering his family history, it's no surprise that Edwin Turner's journey through life consisted of stumbling and zigzagging between depression and rage.

Turner's grandmother and great-grandmother were both committed to mental hospitals on numerous occasions, and his mother attempted suicide twice but failed both times. Turner's father managed to succeed at killing himself, albeit in a highly unusual way; the man fired a shotgun into a shed filled with dynamite, causing an explosion that took his life.

Turner himself seemed fine and well-adjusted until the age of 15, when his mother took the boy to the hospital several times because he was, in her words, "acting funny." Turner was getting bad grades at school, he couldn't sleep at night, and the doctors were worried about his "agitated depression."

At age 18, Turner failed his first suicide attempt. He put the barrel of a rifle in his mouth and tried to pull the trigger, but the gun slipped and Turner only succeeded in blowing off part of his jaw, mouth, and nose. Turner lived, but his face was so disfigured that he began wrapping a white towel around his head, leaving only his eyes visible, whenever he went out in public or spent time with his family and friends.

Five years later, Turner slit his wrists but once again failed to kill himself. He bounced in and out of mental hospitals afterward, his mood fluctuating between happy and sad. One day he would feel so good that he would strip off all his clothes and dance naked in a local bar, then the next day he would spend hours sobbing and criticizing himself for being a bad person.

Shortly after one of his hospital stays, Turner spent an evening drinking beer and smoking pot with his friend Paul Stewart. The two men then cruised around town in Stewart's car for a while, but they eventually swerved off the road and got stuck in a ditch. They walked to the home of a friend, who gave them a ride back to Turner's house, but the two men quickly became bored and decided to commit a robbery.

Armed with high-powered rifles, the men stormed into a nearby truck stop and demanded money. Stewart wore a hockey mask to conceal his identity while Turner's face was hidden by his "signature towel." Turner shot and wounded the store clerk, who fell to the ground. The men then tried to make off with the store's money, but couldn't figure out how to open the cash register. Stewart got frustrated and shot the register, but it remained closed. Turner tried beating the machine with the butt of his rifle, then he fired a shot into it as well. The stubborn register still refused to open. In a fit of rage, Turner shot the store clerk a second time, killing him.

The men then drove to a different truck stop to try again. This time Stewart ordered the store clerk to take the money out of the cash register while Turner stayed in the parking lot to rob a man who had been filling his car with gas. Turner shot and killed the man after stealing his cash, then he and Stewart fled the scene and drove back to Turner's house. After counting and dividing the money from the robbery, which totaled about $400, the two ate a late-night snack of shrimp and cinnamon rolls then went to sleep.

It only took a few hours for police to show up at Turner's home. Why so fast? Well, there were two reasons. First, Turner lived in a small town. Everyone knew about his disfigured face, and customers at the truck stops recognized his "signature towel" immediately. Second, Turner managed to dispel any possible doubt by wearing a jacket that said *Turner* on it when he committed the robberies.

Let me pause for a moment to explain the nature and function of a disguise. First, if you wear some type of camouflage on a daily basis—whether it be a ski mask, a false moustache, or a towel wrapped around your face—then that item effectively loses its power to conceal your identity. The truck stop customers knew exactly who lurked beneath that "signature towel." It would've been like Slash committing a bank robbery wearing that tall black hat, or Michael Jackson gripping a pistol in his sequined glove as he held up a liquor store. Even if Turner had swapped his usual white towel for one of a different color, the witnesses probably wouldn't have been fooled.

Second, wearing an article of clothing with your name stitched on it is always a poor choice during a felony. Clothing with no names is preferable, but if you do feel the need to wear a shirt, jacket, or jersey with a name on it, choose a name other than your own. The police might not fall for your clever hoax, but your chances are still better than if you wear your own name emblazoned across your chest or back. Just imagine how obvious it would be if Eli Manning or Kobe Bryant committed a crime dressed in their uniforms, or if that helpful sales boy from your local retail shop failed to take off his name tag before he launched a campaign of armed robbery.

Prosecutors didn't have a hard time convicting Stewart and Turner of the crimes. Police found the rifles and Stewart's hockey mask at Turner's home, and Stewart made things easier by confessing then testifying against Turner in court. Eyewitnesses also had no problem fingering Turner, who wore his signature towel to court each day in case anybody needed their memory refreshed.

Turner would languish on death row for nearly 17 years before he was finally executed. His lawyers attempted a last-minute stay, claiming that Turner was either mentally ill or mentally retarded. After reading a letter Turner wrote to the New Oxford Review while in prison, though, these claims seem hard to justify. Turner's letter, which concerned media coverage of religious issues, included comments like "I am so bombarded by the Tom Brokaws and Katie Courics and their ilk that at times I question whether I am right about Christ after all," and "I feel so vulnerable that I don't even read my

Time magazine anymore, for fear I may get tricked by its sophistry."

I can't help picturing Turner wearing a smoking jacket and puffing on a pipe as he drafted this elegant letter, perhaps sitting in an overstuffed chair in some comfortable den with books lining the walls and a fire blazing in the hearth. Mentally retarded? I don't think so. Mentally ill? Not unless Turner was Mississippi's version of the Phantom of the Opera, a brilliant, evil genius who could mask his disfigured face but not his disfigured mind. It seems more likely that Turner was simply a man who got drunk, got high, got bored, and then killed two men during an evening of senseless violence.

Before his execution on February 8, 2012, Turner enjoyed a last meal of medium-rare Porterhouse steak, fried shrimp with cocktail sauce, a salad with Russian dressing, Texas toast, iced tea, and a pack of red Twizzlers. The man who combined shrimp and cinnamon rolls after committing his grisly crimes had assembled yet another intriguing meal.

A few hours after he finished eating, Turner was executed in the state penitentiary's lethal injection chamber. Mississippi's most mysterious killer had thrown in the towel at last.

Spotlight On: Loony Last Words

Every condemned prisoner has the chance to say a few final words before they're executed, but that's not always as easy as it sounds. Jerry Seinfeld once remarked that the number one fear in our society is public speaking, with the number two fear being death. Imagine, then, how nervous a person would be if they had to make a speech right before they were executed!

Double murderer James Lee Clark obviously couldn't handle the pressure when asked for his last words. "Uh, I don't know," he mumbled. "Um, I don't know what to say. I don't know." Clark then noticed the witnesses outside the execution chamber for the first time and added, "I didn't know anybody was there. Howdy."

But not every killer gets tongue-tied in their final moments. Some confess their crimes, recite religious scripture, or apologize to their victim's families. A few even make jokes or lighthearted remarks.

I've been hanging around this popsicle stand way too long, I want to tell you all. When I die, bury me deep, lay two speakers at my feet, put some headphones on my head, and rock 'n' roll me when I'm dead. I'll see you in heaven someday. —Douglas Roberts

Tell the governor he just lost my vote. Y'all hurry this along, I'm dying to get out of here. —Christopher Scott Emmett

Where's a stunt double when you need one? —Vincent Gutierrez

Some clever convicts make puns involving their names, such as these three men who all died in the electric chair.

Well, gentlemen, you are about to see a baked Appel. —George Appel

Gents, this is an educational project. You are about to witness the damaging effect electricity has on Wood. —Frederick Wood

Death Row's Oddest Inmates

Hey, fellas! How about this for a headline for tomorrow's paper? 'French Fries.' —James French

Some inmates take the opportunity to praise their favorite sports teams. While you'll rarely find references to baseball, basketball, or hockey, condemned prisoners seem wildly passionate about football teams with dismal performance records.

Go Raiders! —Robert Comer

The Raiders are going all the way, y'all. —John Albert Burks

When the Browns are in the Super Bowl in the next five years, you'll know I'm up there doing my magic. —James Filiaggi

Redskins are going to the Super Bowl. —Bobby Lee Ramdass

What about those Cowboys? —William Prince Davis

I am thankful to the Dallas Cowboys for giving me a lot of enjoyment these past years. —Earl Behringer

Not all last words are this light and breezy. Some inmates vent their anger, even if it's unclear who they're angry at.

I am not guilty of the charge of capital murder. Steal me and my family's money. My truth will always be my truth. There is no kin and no friend; no fear what you do to me. No kin to you, undertaker. Murderer. Go to hell. Get my money. Give me my rights. Give me my rights. Give me my rights. Give me my life back. —Kelsey Patterson

Others know exactly who they're mad at and aren't afraid to drop names.

I just want everyone to know that the prosecutor and Bill Scott are sorry sons of bitches. —Edward Ellis

Somebody needs to kill my trial attorney. —George Harris

I hope you rot in hell, bitch. I hope you fucking rot in hell, bitch. You bitch. I hope you fucking rot, cunt. That is it. —Cameron Todd Willingham (addressing his ex-wife)

A few hours ago, Wayne Snow said I had no redeeming qualities. The only thing I've got to say to Wayne Snow is kiss my ass. Bye. —William Mitchell (Snow was chairman of the state pardons board)

Variations of the ass-kissing theme have appeared many times over the years, including the following:

Kiss my ass. You'll never find the rest! —John Wayne Gacy (referring to the bodies of his undiscovered victims)

To all of the racist white folks in America that hate black folks, and to all of the black folks in America that hate themselves, the infamous words of my famous, legendary brother Nat Turner; y'all kiss my black ass. Let's do it. — Brian Roberson

I'd like to thank my family for loving me and taking care of me. And the rest of the world can kiss my ever-loving ass, because I'm innocent. —Johnny Frank Garrett

Remember this. If all you know is hatred, if all you know is blood love, you'll never be satisfied. For everybody out there that is like that and knows nothing but negative, kiss my proud white Irish ass. —Robert Atworth

Last but not least, some killers have chosen to end their lives with a gesture rather than words. As Donald Harding was being put to death in Arizona's gas chamber, he struggled against his forearm straps in a desperate attempt to give the state attorney general, who was witnessing the execution, the middle finger.

Fellow Arizona inmate Jimmie Wayne Jeffers succeeded in flipping off his executioners, and the digit remained extended even after Jeffers was declared dead.

But Reginald Brooks, sentenced to death in Ohio for killing his own three sons, elevated the art of the "last gesture" to new heights. As the lethal injection drugs began to take effect, Brooks managed to raise the middle fingers of both hands so he could flip off the prison officials inside the death chamber and the execution witnesses outside the chamber, too. As with Jeffers, the two fingers stood tall even after Brooks was dead—proving that even the state government can't kill two birds with one stone.

###

About the Author

Ty Treadwell is the co-author of *Last Suppers: Famous Final Meals from Death Row*.

His suspense and horror stories have appeared in Writer's Journal, Unreality, Over My Dead Body, and many other magazines. These can now be found in the collection *Down a Crooked Road; Tales of Mystery & Suspense*. Treadwell is also the author of *The Devil Did Grin*, a mystery novel.

Over the course of his career, Treadwell has also sold over 150 articles and essays. His awards include a gold medal in the essay category at the 2008 GAMMA Awards and first prize in the 2007 Travel Writing Contest sponsored by Writer's Journal. He once taught writing classes for Clayton State University and now teaches an online writing class that attracts students from across the country.

Also by Ty Treadwell

Last Suppers: Famous Final Meals from Death Row
by Ty Treadwell & Michelle Vernon

One death row inmate requested 24 tacos, 6 enchiladas, and 6 tostadas. Another wanted wild rabbit, biscuits, and blackberry pie. And a two-time murderer asked for a can of SpaghettiOs then complained to the press when he didn't get it!

Newly revised and updated, this 10th anniversary edition contains dozens of intriguing last meals ranging from succulent steak and lobster to the lump of dirt ordered by a former voodoo priest. But Last Suppers is more than just a list of meals; you'll also be treated to weird execution facts, prison recipes, and other tidbits of trivia from America's toughest cell blocks. Ever wondered how the last meal tradition began, or what the most popular entrees are among condemned diners? Curious about the lives and loves of capital punishment's fairer sex, the Death Row Dames? Are you craving a taste of Texas Jailhouse Chili, but don't have the recipe? Dying to know what Ted Bundy, John Wayne Gacy, and other famous serial killers ate before their demise? Then pull up a chair, tuck in that bib, and enjoy!

The Devil Did Grin
by Ty Treadwell

Some people say *When life gives you lemons, make lemonade*. Will Deacon says, *When life gives you lemons, throw those lemons back at life as hard as you can, and if life ends up with bumps on its head and lemon juice in its eye, it really can't complain because it's the one that gave you those stupid lemons in the first place.*

Former private detective Will Deacon is jobless, aimless, and hasn't traveled more than two blocks from his Atlanta condo in nearly a year—but he's never been happier. A survivor of countless failed careers and one and a half failed marriages, Will is perfectly content to stay holed up at home with only a cat named Socrates for company. But that blissful life comes to an end when the son of an old friend commits suicide. The pampered teen had no reason to kill himself, so Will is dragged out of retirement to find the answer. As he delves into the boy's hidden lifestyle, Will finds himself up against a sleek drug dealer, two frightening hit men, and the head of the Dixie Mafia. When the evidence points to murder instead of suicide, Will is caught in a whirlwind of shocking discoveries and dark family secrets as he tries to solve the most important case of his career.

Down a Crooked Road:
Tales of Mystery & Suspense
by Ty Treadwell

Take the last sharp turn on a crooked road and you might find yourself face to face with a desperate killer, or a clever con man, or a restless spirit whose face is eerily familiar. In the tradition of The Twilight Zone, the 12 stories in this collection all share one common trait; each one ends with a delicious, unexpected twist.

In "The Woman Upstairs," a claustrophobic housewife uses extreme measures to escape from both a cramped apartment and a confining marriage. "The Sorrow Business" tells how a devious reporter suffers the consequences after hounding a murder victim's family for an interview. And in "Deep in the Roaring Fork," a man lost in the backwoods of Colorado stumbles across a lonely tavern whose bartender knows far too many details about his life — and about his death. Includes 7 stories previously published in mystery magazines like *Over My Dead Body* and *Unreality*, as well as 5 brand new stories from award-winning writer Ty Treadwell.

Find Ty Treadwell on the web at:

www.tytreadwell.com

www.lastsuppersbook.blogspot.com

www.deathrowsoddestinmates.blogspot.com

Printed in Poland
by Amazon Fulfillment
Poland Sp. z o.o., Wrocław